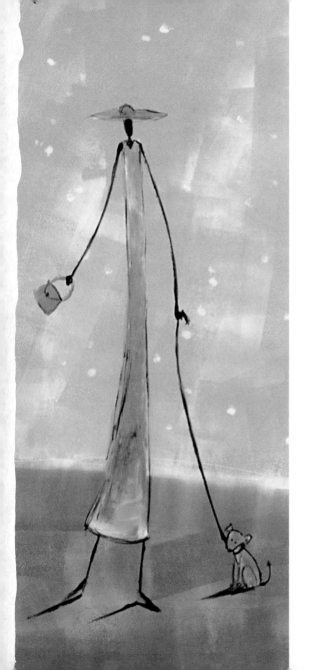

# City Girl
## Philosophy

Everything You Need to Live
a Simply Stunning Life

*Words & Art*

## Karn Knutson

Conari Press

First published in 2007 by Conari Press,
an imprint of Red Wheel/Weiser, LLC
With offices at:
500 Third Street, Suite 230
San Francisco, CA 94107
*www.redwheelweiser.com*

ISBN-10: 1-57324-287-X
ISBN-13: 978-1-57324-287-5
Library of Congress Cataloging-in-Publication Data
available upon request

Cover and book design by Karn Knutson
Typeset in Perpetua and Savoye
Cover illustration © Karn Knutson

Printed in China
CC
10 9 8 7 6 5 4 3 2 1

# Pretty Pieces of Your City Girl World

# Oh, to Be a City Girl!

Isn't life wonderful knowing every flower is growing just for you?

The City Girl Philosophy is everything a City Girl should know about shoes, love, friends, fun, men, careers, shopping, and all other things needed to live a simply stunning life.

A City Girl breezes through her days, bounding from handsome man to shoe store, always looking fabulous. She would love to meet you for lunch as long as the café doesn't clash with her ensemble. She will even save you a seat in the good lighting, unless of course, there's only room for one.

Her style is discernable from head to toe, though it is far more than her clothes. Naturally, they are stunning, but it is her view of the world, which is all her own—and very well color coordinated.

To be a City Girl and live an "Oh, so fabulous!" life, there are simply things that *must* be—strong martinis, strong men, even stronger women, and your hat, shoes, bag, and dog should *always* match.

A City Girl knows your best friends are the ones who make you laugh until you snort. Not at all crass, as long as your martini does not come out your nose.

She has the perfect attitude for all situations:

SHOPPING: When?
DESSERTS: Yes, thank you.
CAREERS: Expense account lunches.
BOYS: Yummy.
MARTINIS: Dry.
SENSE OF HUMOR: Dry.
KISSES: Just a little wet.

To live in a City Girl world is not just where you live—it's a state of mind. You can actually be a City Girl if you have a yard larger than a window box or even have seen a cow in real life.

Bold, beautiful, daring, fascinating, fantastic—if there is a word that describes being enviable in any way, it describes being a City Girl. She is a palatable princess and a delightful diva.

Like a well-cut diamond, a City Girl has many facets, each one brilliant. She knows the least she can do is share her wonderfulness with the world as it revolves around her. But as brightly as her fabulousness may shine, it never singes. A rude City Girl is simply rude, and soon tarnishes her own appeal.

## Your hat, shoes, bag, and dog should always match.

She agrees practicality can be a wonderful thing, as long as it doesn't interfere with things looking good. A City Girl tends to choose form over function. **If the dress looks good, it doesn't matter if it's larger than the car that's taking you to the party. That's what limos are for.**

### However, Bigger isn't always better.

Expense accounts, closets, and slices of cake – *Yes.*

Debts, heartbreaks, or your hair – *No.*

The City Girl Philosophy shares diamonds and pearls of wisdom about being divine and helps answer nagging little questions like: Why am I so fabulous? Is there such a thing as too many shoes? Who invented bad lighting, and can we have him arrested?

So, if you are confident in being a little "girly," a little naughty, and completely divine, let the City Girl Philosophy assist you in making your life a bit more fabulous, with a City Girl view of how things should be.

# Life Is a Runway

    A City Girl starts every day with the bare essential of life: not being bare. Whether your closet is walk-in, crammed-in, or in its own wing, greet it with a smile you would give your dearest friend. After all, this is your arsenal for outfitting, wardrobing, costuming, and putting the hot in hottie, but with style far beyond her fashion—even when bare, a City Girl's style is still there.

    Luckily, having style isn't only the pleasure of City Girls with gobs of money. Money doesn't buy taste—just look at Vegas—and cheap doesn't mean bad. (Unless you're referring to your date, or worse, your date's cologne. Ewh!) But, cheap does not mean good. Good means good, and good and cheap means lucky. So why not buy two?

*Having a signature style* often involves a signature color, but always in moderation. A City Girl loves to have her world match, but never in a matchy-matchy way. Looking like a freshly dipped egg is, oh, so unappealing. Even if you love the color, wearing it head to toe may cause onlookers to use words like banana, blue bird, or green giant in reference to your appearance. These are not good things.

As well as she knows "Wow!" a City Girl has a keen eye for subtle and knows there is a myriad of possibilities within any hue. For example, the category of Light Pink is really so much more: there's Pale, Blush, Pale-Pale, Hint, Morning Dew, Powder Puff, even Hint-of-the-Idea-of-Pink. However, this concept of color does not apply to beige. One can barely say the word without forming an expression to match.

Beige is dull, bland, and blah. It's the color of things that don't have enough sense to have a real name. So, never wear beige. Ever. In a world where you can have buff, cream, ecru, fawn, neutral, sand, stone, tawny, or taupe, why? Oh, why? Would you settle for calling anything beige? Unless maybe to describe the personality of an ex.

*Never wear beige. Ever.*

A City Girl's eye also knows when things are close but not quite. This is especially important in the area of black. Trying to get away with a good black, paired with a one-too-many-times-at-the-cleaners black is always an Oops. Exception: You haven't made it to the cleaners, and it is your only option other than a teal sequined bolero jacket that's still hiding in the back of your closet taking up valuable real estate. To avoid this, simply stop for a bit of shopping any time the dry cleaner is so foolish as to not be open when you've arrived.

# Concerning closet space: It's like

air, you can't live without it, and it's better if it's clean. If your wardrobe is choking on last season's not-working-this-season items and articles that have erroneous, if not ridiculous emotional attachments, you can barely breathe, let alone put together something divine.

This is exactly why periodically pruning your closet is needed. An ensemble purge creates empty hangers, which is good for two reasons: (1) A few empty hangers will keep you from ever feeling the slightest bit guilty for having too many clothes—as if you could. And (2)

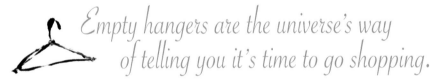

*Empty hangers are the universe's way of telling you it's time to go shopping.*

Closet slimming cannot only cure things that are out of style, but out of fit. Occasionally, clothes have the audacity to stop being your size. When things stop fitting you perfectly, don't fight with them, just break up, let go, and go shopping. The same goes for men.

# New Treasure Acquisition (a.k.a. Shopping)

While a City Girl believes in taking risks, even fashion ones, she never shops in desperation, even if there is an invite in hand and no cute in the closet. It causes things like teal sequined bolero jackets to happen.

Avoiding frantic shopping is the perfect reason to buy cute little party clothes when you find them, even if you have no immediate need for them.

## Take risks, even fashion ones.

Even if you have nine little black dresses at home, you can never really have too many. If one slinks in all the right places, and one shows just the right amount of curve, knee, or cleave, it serves its own purpose in your wardrobe, and it makes Basic Black anything but basic.

Also, avoid bad fashion moments by only ever shopping with good friends and good lighting. If you're without one, you most definitely must have the other.

Now, when a City Girl shops, she is always looking for the perfect size. Of course, **the perfect size is the one you're wearing whenever you are happy, regardless of the number on the tag.** Tags itch anyway, so a little careful work with the scissors takes care of both issues.

Speaking of issues, fashion magazines are delicious for dreaming, but a City Girl never judges herself against their glossy pages. She knows real life doesn't come with retouching, and dessert is far too fun to give up. Not to mention, it's cumbersome having three stylists and a lighting expert following you all day. A City Girl may have a fantasy life, but she's happy being fantastic in her reality.

Another reason to look at glossy pages with a discerning eye is that a City Girl's perfect look can only be achieved when she starts with style, not fad. Just because a designer was "inspired" doesn't mean you will be. And everyone having something doesn't make it wonderful—it makes it on the verge of passé.

# What to Wear?

Shopping for anything is really shopping for compliments. Also, this is very different than fishing for them. Fishing is tacky. Simply be your wonderful City Girl self and you'll get them naturally. Or, give them to yourself if no one else with good taste is around.

*Never be flattered by a compliment from someone who can't match their own clothing.*

This includes sales associates. They may be overwhelmed by your stylish presence, and tell you something looks fabulous when really it only makes you look wonderful. Close, but why settle when you're capable of so much more?

Once your closet is filled with fabulous, there are all sorts of reasons to dress up, down, over-the-top, or simply not. The one occasion that can seem perplexing is: How to dress for men? This is really a trick question, because a City Girl always dresses for herself, or occasionally, for the rest of the girls if a new clothing demonstration is on the itinerary. A City Girl's approach to all wardrobe selections is whatever makes her feel divine, whatever the look she's going for.

Granted, some of your clothing choices may have very specific intentions, such as getting his attention or making him drool, but those are still for your benefit. Thus, for you. Men get to enjoy gazing upon your fabulousness in everything you wear—even less if they're really lucky, so they should be happy. The good ones know this, along with many synonyms for beautiful to show they know this.

Occasionally, tell a man you wore something just for him—it makes him feel special and get all puffy-chested. It's cute.

# Accessories (a.k.a. Necessities)

The most flattering thing any City Girl can wear is confidence—it's even better than something sparkly. Remember, the true function of any accessory is to draw more attention to you, not itself. Even a deliciously huge diamond should only be as beautiful as you are, not more.

Thankfully there are many categories for adding a little something, and all should do their best to make you look yours.

SHOES: If you must have them, and have nothing to go with them, it is a sign that you have more shopping to do.

HATS: Everyone can wear them. It has nothing to do with how they look, it's the attitude they give you, and the attitude you can give others. Keep in mind, if you are a City Girl of the fussy-hair variety, be careful with your choice of chapeau and occasions for wearing them. Hat-hair, unlike hats, hardly works on anyone.

JEWELRY: Sparkly, shiny, just the right touch—All good. Clunky, noisy, made of macaroni—Not so good.

BAGS: Being called a bag lady is fine as long as they're talking about Gucci. A "bag" can refer to a multitude of cute things designed to carry other cute things, from a catch-all large enough to fit your life into to something that barely holds anything but air.

The essential "purse" refers to the medium, small, tiny, and minute range of bags. The last most often occurs for dates. Typically being required to carry little else than air. A good guide: Your "purse" should be able to fit in your "bag." And your "date purse" can usually fit in your date's pocket.

 TAILORS (a.k.a. Magicians): Neither "binding" nor "bagging" belong in a City Girl's clothing vocabulary.

CLEANERS: Same as tailors, but for spots and dinge.

EYEWEAR: If the point is to see and be seen, don't let vanity catch you squinting. Needing glasses can be cumbersome, even ugly if you let it. So, absolutely don't let it.

A City Girl treats glasses like shoes—she has styles and colors to fit her moods, seasons, and shoes. Glam works, and intellectual is always handy. An added benefit: Sliding your specs on, or taking them off with flare adds dramatic pause to anything you say. Plus, it draws more attention to your face—always a good thing.

Eyewear of the sunglass variety is anything but a bother, except when you leave them in the limo. Every City Girl knows a world of privacy and glamour lives behind that glorious UV coating. Not to mention, they eliminate that nasty squinting.

ALL OTHER THINGS OUTFIT ADDITIONAL: If Prada would only make a shopping cart, even getting groceries could be stylish. This category can include outerwear, dates, restaurants, pets, vehicles, even family members. Generally choose them to compliment your handbag. Literally. If they can speak, they should be saying nice things as well as not clashing. Note: This can be a tricky area—loved ones don't always agree to changing when *their* clothes don't match *your* shoes.

HAIRWEAR: This is easy: No Crissy Snow. No birds or fruit. No adding hair that they can tell didn't start there.

MISSING BUT NEVER MISSED: One City Girl accessory that is a must is what she doesn't have—panty lines. Never make your booty a "Boo." Thong it, bare it, or Lycra derriere it, but please, just do not crease it.

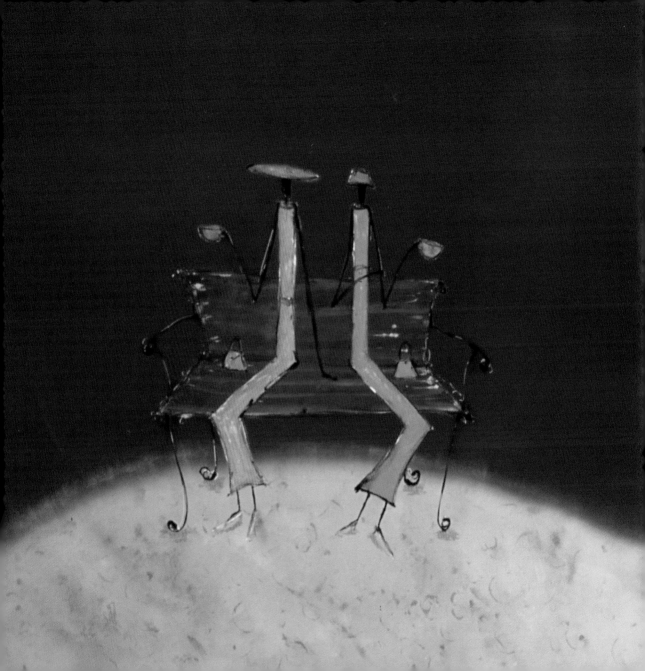

# My Closet Is Your Closet

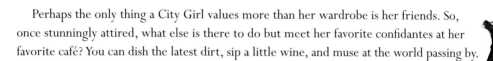

Perhaps the only thing a City Girl values more than her wardrobe is her friends. So, once stunningly attired, what else is there to do but meet her favorite confidantes at her favorite café? You can dish the latest dirt, sip a little wine, and muse at the world passing by.

## When people watching, be at least as interesting to watch.

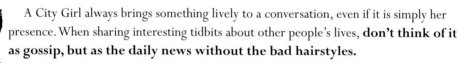

A City Girl always brings something lively to a conversation, even if it is simply her presence. When sharing interesting tidbits about other people's lives, **don't think of it as gossip, but as the daily news without the bad hairstyles.**

For the answer to any question, a City Girl knows to ask "The Girls." These are the fabulous women who inhabit the inner of your inner circle, your very best, best friends. They are your trusted advisors who always have brilliant opinions on any topic. You may never be positive about a solution, but you'll have divine company while discussing the world's great problems—politics, hunger, not having the right shoes for your date on Friday.

Occasionally, "The Girls" can include boys. These are most often boys who like boys, but once in a while, a straight one earns his way in.

The best straight male version of One-of-the-Girls is a man you've known for years, but have never dated, hooked up, or slept with. These friendships are ideal for both of you because a City Girl is perfect for a single boy to invite along when shopping for . . . anything really, but especially furniture and clothes. These are things he hopes will impress a City Girl of his own, who he's hoping you will introduce him to. The benefit for a City Girl: more shopping, and he can't complain about carrying the bags.

# How to Tell a True Friend

- First, you can tell her anything. Even the things too embarrassing to tell anyone, but too good to not tell someone. So, who better?
- She lets you borrow her clothes, even when you look better in them than she does.
- Offers you a shoulder to cry on. Even when she's wearing silk and isn't sure your mascara is waterproof.
- She won't let you buy anything when you make her promise not to, then will shop with you in complete futility, telling you that you looked incredible in everything, but nothing was fabulous enough to buy.
- Knows your favorite candy for good days, your favorite Ben & Jerry's for the bad ones, and your preferred cocktail for all the rest.

*Can seamlessly rationalize a shared dessert into any meal.*

- Will still act silly when you're both too old to keep your teeth in when laughing.
- She will run, walk, or ride however many Ks you need her to for whichever cause you have deemed worthy. Even if it changes every month. Even if her fancy new running clothes look adorable, but fit terribly, and chafe in action. (Something not revealed in the fitting room.)
- Her phone calls are accepted at any time, even in inconvenient places. Yes, flushing may be heard.
- She will meet you for lunch, even when she's just eaten, because there is always dessert. Besides, if either of you has new purchases to show off, why wait?

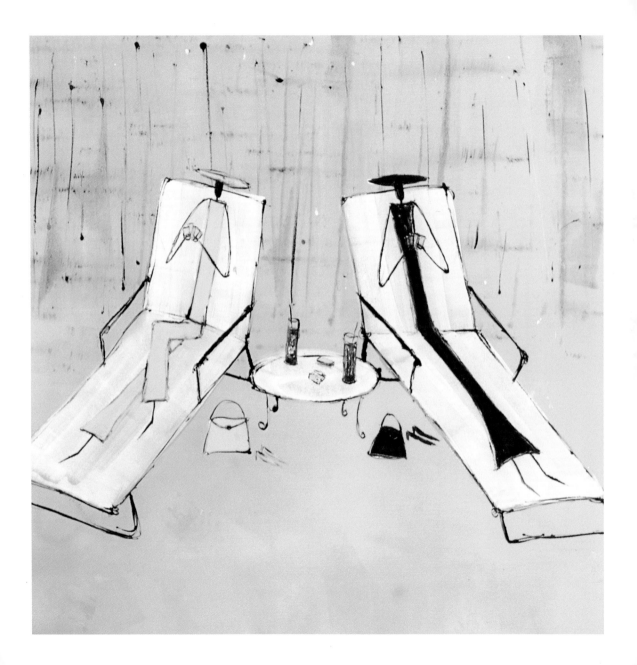

# Borrowing Etiquette

When evaluating a friend's latest wardrobe acquisition, consider how it looks on her, but don't forget to consider its borrowability—a.k.a. how it will look on you.

- It is never okay to talk someone into buying something just so you can borrow it.
- Do not borrow before they've debuted it themselves. Unless, however, three months have passed and it's hanging lonely in her closet, and it's nearly out of season. At that point it's the least you can do, it's nearly charitable. Plus, it will look so good on you.
- A round trip borrow involves a layover at the cleaners.

## Never merely sniff and say, "Okay."

- When complimented, which of course you will be, give credit for your friend's impeccable taste. Exception: If the person complimenting you is snotty, then say a mild "Thank you" and shrug it off as just another of the many fabulous things you possess.
- Replace the "Oops." Replace meaning same or better, and picking up lunch while shopping for it. Remember, a City Girl is always reasonable while finding equivalents. Accidents are not lotteries. Asking for a second glass of wine for your mental anguish is fine, asking for Manolos to match is not.

# ·:: Girls' Night ::·

The only thing better than getting together with one amazing friend is City Girls en masse—a.k.a. Girls' Night. When planning, there is really no need for one, but a reason for Girls' Night can determine the amount of wine needed or how much stretch you should have in your denim.

*Note: Menu planning for Girls' Night.*
*Veggie tray: No. Gooey, Cheesy, Chocolaty,*
*"Please don't tell me what's in this": Yes, yes, yes!*

## Always good reasons for Girls' Night:

- Someone needs to vent.
- Everyone needs to vent.
- Boys get boring. Usually why everyone is venting.
- You have a corkscrew and know how to use it.
- You've purged your closet, and there are garments in need of good homes.

For inconceivable reasons, there can be things in your closet that no matter how adorable or sexy they should be, they never look quite right on you. Hard to believe. **Thankfully, one City Girl's camel-toe causing, hottie jeans can give another City Girl a booty to die for.** Plus, reshopping provides great entertainment and compliment-giving opportunities.

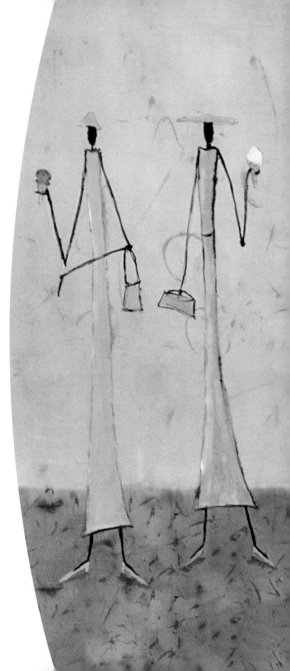

# "Ooh, That Looks Yummy!"

A City Girl will eat anywhere that doesn't clash with her shoes. Of course, not clashing with her requires exquisite taste and fabulous presentation. She especially loves sidewalk cafés on sunny days. They are like little stages, and perfect for lunch with a side of hat and sunglasses.

When choosing restaurants, stars can be handy recommendation devices. Both the pointy sort printed in the review columns as well as the two-legged, big-ego kind that fill the gossip column. The more of either any eatery has is a good thing.

Hole-in-the-wall or linen-and-crystal? Both can be delicious. The first may restrict your choice of footwear to the closed-toe variety—they often have random things you can step in.

## *A City Girl will eat anywhere that doesn't clash with her shoes.*

Wherever you choose to dine, remember: Entrees are like shoes, if three options satisfy you for different reasons, you simply must take your time deciding. This is what the first bottle of wine is for. However, unlike shoes you can't simply order all three, but a City Girl can persuade her tablemates to order her other choices, then they can share. If not, definitely choose better companions.

### *Keep in mind when you "share" the yummy selections of others:*

- Ask first. Exception: French fries are communal property.
- Take only one bite. Okay, two at most if it's really good, or dessert.
- Absolutely do not insist on seasoning their food.

Speaking of Yummy, a City Girl never pretends to not eat. No matter who's across the table from her, she eats. She loves food. Sometimes a City Girl even likes bad food. Not bad tasting—that's never acceptable, but bad that's not good for you. Gooey, rich, fried, things on sticks, anything in the ice cream, whipped cream, or double cream category. A City Girl knows dessert can come first, or be the meal. **However, supersizing is a concept that should be reserved for diamonds, never dinner.**

# Calling All Chefs

If for some reason you're not going to dine out every evening, spending time in the kitchen allows a City Girl to appreciate why she tips so well. **Plus, cookbooks are great for finding new things to order when you are out.**

When venturing near appliances, choose clothing that can withstand splatters. Aprons are an option if worn with enough City Girl sass to transcend their kitsch. And strangely, kitchens not only make clogs acceptable, but cool. Go figure.

Remember, cooking is a wonderful thing—to have done for you. When you actually do cook, be fearless, keep an extinguisher handy, and have discreet delivery on speed dial for those trials that are errors. Thankfully, cooking has a wide spectrum of definitions for a City Girl, everything from "From Scratch" to "Hide the Containers."

A City Girl can be an expert gourmet without even knowing how to sauté. It's all about developing your skills of arranging the takeout on pretty plates, stealthily disposing of the evidence, and keeping a straight face while omitting bits of the story. Such as: "I made the call to get it here" becomes, "I made it." See, simple.

# Straight Up, Two Olives

Something a City Girl knows as well as her wardrobe is her cocktails, and this knowledge begins with knowing how to hold one.

A martini glass can be tricky. Hold it gingerly with a nonchalant air. A City Girl's hand cradles the glass, showing off her nails, never daintily pinching the stem. A variation of that skill is reserved for wine, but with cocktails, you command the glass.

*Nondripping swizzle sticks provide extra hand-gesture flare.*

Mind how you mix cocktails with hand gestures—keep the gestures to your free hand to avoid spillage. It's wasteful, and wasting a well-mixed cocktail is like wearing stilettos to do the laundry. However, used correctly, a little spill, and an "Oops, did I get you?" allows for introductions and physique inspection while dabbing the pectorals of a well-chosen spill recipient.

Securely skewered garnishes or nondripping swizzle sticks provide extra hand-gesture flare, and sliding a vodka-soaked olive off with your tongue can be very effective for gaining a man's attention. Mind you, it can also cause him to completely lose his train of thought, so use your weapons wisely. If his story is interesting, hold off. If he is talking incessantly, and it's not about how amazing you are, fire away.

Now, for what to hold. If you're in the mood to experiment, or coordinate, you're in luck. Cocktails come in all sorts of fun flavors and corresponding colors. However, a City Girl knows rainbows are pretty in the sky, but drinking one may leave you looking like a puddle.

# Hooray for Me, and You. But Really Me.

Entertaining starts with entering, and making a great entrance is a key skill for any City Girl. It is how she lets the guests know she has arrived, so they can get excited and the party can truly begin.

A City Girl may completely captivate a room but never make anyone feel inferior, even if they are. After all, it's not her fault if the world pales in her presence.

*Things to remember for making a City Girl worthy entrance:*

- Don't trip.
- Smile. Your teeth should be free of lipstick, spinach, or any descriptor less than dazzling.
- Hold your head high, as if wearing a tiara. Or, if you are wearing a tiara, smooth a bit of your hair, so everyone will look in that direction.
- Walk or glide with a little pause, as if looking for someone, which you are. A well-executed entrance allows you to survey the prospects. This way you will never miss an opportunity to make lingering eye contact with any potentially interesting boys.

*Occasionally, exit a room for simply no other reason than to make another entrance.*

#  Why a Party? Why Not, Silly?

While a City Girl's daily life is delicious, there's always room to turn good into very, very good. So, why not have a party? Some days are obvious party occasions, like birthdays.

## A City Girl simply doesn't understand why her birthday isn't a national holiday.

Thankfully, not every party requires a purpose of such magnitude. Really, any reason will do. Having one can determine the color scheme for the invitations and whether someone other than you will be the center of attention. Well, more accurately, who will be sharing a sliver of your spotlight.

### CITY GIRL-WORTHY REASONS FOR CELEBRATIONS:

- You found the perfect party dress and it feels unfulfilled.
- You've done something more brilliant than usual at work.
- Showing off a new boyfriend.
- Showing off that you've gotten rid of the old boyfriend.
- Something good happening to a friend. (This may require more than merely sharing. Full spotlight relinguishment may be called for.)
- Something bad happened to a friend and she wishes to forget about it. *Note: Order more Vodka.*

Having a party for a non-reason reason works perfectly well also. A City Girl never worries about rationale being rational. The classic non-reason for a party reason: your house needs to be cleaned. The fear of public humiliation via dust bunnies will force you to get reacquainted with your broom. Or, like any good City Girl, the cleaning service you have on speed dial. Rubber gloves go with so few outfits.

Some things are a bit less grand and do not require a full-blown party to celebrate. Things like a friend losing the three pounds only she can see. Even if it's the third time she has reachieved her goal, it deserves celebration. A hug, well-mixed cocktail, or chocolate bits do nicely. Of course, some celebrations tend to be the reason for the reachieving.

# Who, Where, When?

Once you plan to have a party, you must plan the party. This involves many choices, the height of heel you'll be wearing is only the beginning.

CHOOSING DECORATIONS: When planning a party, start with your outfit. Then you'll know what color the decorations need to be.

CHOOSING A DATE: This refers to both categories, each requiring careful consideration. (1) The day, week, and month affect your wardrobe options. (2) What man will be accessorizing your arm affects the number of cocktails required to make him interesting.

CHOOSING GUESTS: This is simple. Invite anyone who is fabulous, funny, or brilliant, and no one who is creepy in any way, has a penchant for complaining, or is just dull. Avoiding the dull tends to be easy. They're dull, thus easy to forget. Unlike yourself.

CHOOSING A LOCATION: The size of venue required for your soiree comes down to two things. (1) Will your party dress wrinkle terribly in an overflowing cocktail lounge? and (2) will there be dancing? Unless you're going for a mosh pit sort of thing (Note: No. Emphatically, no!), shaking your booty requires enough room to allow for full appreciation of said booty.

# Party Eats

Once you have Why, Who, Where, and When answered, only What remains. What will the menu be?

*The beverage portion is simple—full bar, full cellar, and a store that delivers.*

*Determining party eats has a few more options to choose from:*

- It's your favorite food. If the guests have any taste, they'll like it too. If not, their next invitation gets "lost in the mail."
- Dainty to eat. No unsightly chewing or balancing on the lap. Plus, anything toothpick-skewered only requires one hand, which allows for martini occupation of the other.
- It looked yummy in the cookbook and the caterer knows how to make it.
- Anything easily passing for you having made it yourself.
- Matches your party dress. You can never be too coordinated.
- If your guests or the occasion are so spectacular to warrant a meal involving sitting, the menu should be determined for its visual appeal on the plate—a.k.a. it doesn't leave ugly bits or sloppiness when finished.

# Expense account lunches —or dinner, or drinks,

or clients who prefer to discuss profits over pedicures—it's all good. After all, the paycheck that pays for Prada has to come from somewhere.

It's been said that if work was fun, we'd call it something else. So, let's.

Do you refer to something as important as your crimson, four-inch, strappy sandals with the jeweled buckles as just "shoes"? No. So, why not give your "work" the style it deserves? After all, if you're doing it, it must be fabulous. It's your profession, career, current gig, starring role, maybe even your source of bliss or true calling.

Doing what you absolutely love is the best profession to choose. However, some dream jobs simply don't exist, and openings for "Trust Fund Babies" don't come up very often.

# Beyond that, there are other ways to define your career satisfaction and reasons for a City Girl to tote a business card. And not just that fabulous platinum card case you've been eyeing.

REWARDS: When choosing, or choosing to keep, a particular profession, rewards are best big, frequent, or flattering. Or, deliciously, all three. Keep in mind, monetary rewards always affect your level of living a fabulously color-coordinated life. In an ideal City Girl world, incomes would be proportionate to the amount of beauty and joy one brings to the world.

CHALLENGE: Your brain is as brilliant as your style, so letting it be seen and sharpened is a must. Plus, brilliant moments are ideal for eyewear flair demonstrations.

FULFILLMENT: Whether your career of choice consists of changing lives, changing the world, or simply being able to change your wardrobe every season, your profession should wear your passion as well as you wear those four-inch strappy sandals.

DREAMS: Having found your dream career, your dream office, or your dream boss—You—your City Girl day job should provide the means to live your daydreams and not disturb your night ones. After all, it is called *beauty sleep* for a reason.

# Business Fabulous

Believe it or not, looking good in business isn't just about looking good.

- "Fake it 'til you make it." A City Girl is always confident, even if she has no idea what is going on. A rarity, of course. Look at asking questions like wearing white jeans. If you do either with complete confidence, no one will question.
- Leading by example applies to most everything. Especially dressing. As for business casual, couture is casual if you wear it well.
- Know the difference between confidence and condescension. Always speak with the first, and only occasionally the latter.

## Make requests graciously, demands even more so.

- Accept responsibility as well as you accept a gift. Like the ones in those little blue boxes from Tiffany's.
- Don't point fingers unless you're pointing out a smart ensemble—either clothing or personnel.
- Treat those under you with the respect you would your Gucci luggage. The corporate ladder has been known to skip a rung or two, and your junior could be your senior faster than culottes went out of style. And yes, they are out. I don't care what any designer says, their pronunciation is the only thing "cool" about them.

## Key points to keep in mind, whatever your profession:
- When you're the boss, don't be bossy.
- When you're trying to be the boss, don't be bitchy.
- When you're trying to do the boss, think twice.
  This almost never works out well.

# Elements of a City Girl Career

WARDROBE: When choosing professions, a City Girl looks for things that require a smart wardrobe, preferably one where her shoes are visible.

POLITICS: Being savvy at office politics does not mean you're the go-to person for office gossip. Gossip can be delicious, just like rich, gooey caramel, but it too will stick to you, and too much will make you ill.

PROMOTIONS: If you're not already running the company, it's likely you soon will be. So, never be surprised when your paycheck or title expands. Unlike a waistline, these are good things. Luckily for City Girls of the phobic variety, the corporate ladder can be climbed without fear of heights.

BUSINESS TRAVEL: This is the ugly stepsister to leisure travel. However, any trip is reason to shop, and clients tend to prefer their meals with more stars—both varieties. Big drawback: Not all clients have the good sense to be headquartered in Paris or Bali.

OFFICE DÉCOR: Your desk should never hide your shoes and always have room for your hat. Office space for flowers is a must. A bouquet can inspire a theme color for your week's wardrobe.

A stunning office is a cue to anyone entering, saying, "Yes, I am fabulous and brilliant." And subliminally, it will let them understand your position on "polite conversation": People should be polite and not bore you with their conversation.

# Shall We Meet?

Regardless of your chosen profession, there are always meetings, for which a City Girl has three positions: Avoiding, Attending, or Commanding.

AVOIDING: Bad meetings can be easily identified.
- The snack selection is stale.
- The chairs are uncomfortable.
- The main purpose can be described as, "So he can hear himself speak."
- The attending IQs are questionable. (Never have meetings with stupid people. The frustration can cause your forehead to crease.)

ATTENDING: Meetings, like dates, are a privilege of your presence. Take into consideration its purpose.
- Does it benefit your projects?
- Will your presence benefit others? Okay, this one is a given.
- Is it interfering with something more important on your day's itinerary? Keep in mind, classifying a facial as more important than a budget review with the CEO may have a positive effect on your complexion but a negative one on your ability to continue getting facials.

COMMANDING: This is most often the appropriate place for a City Girl to be in any meeting for two reasons.
- Being in charge of meetings demonstrates her brains and wit. The truly wise around you already know how brilliant you are. For the others, if they're not smart enough to grasp it, again, no meetings with stupid people.
- In addition to your brilliance, the best place to display your stunning attire is in front of a crowd. Just avoid getting caught in projection lighting—it's never flattering, and it causes you to squint, which can be permanently unflattering.

# Maintenance & Self-Sparkling

Never put off pampering yourself. This class of activities should refer to the wonderfully delicious way you treat yourself on a daily basis. So, don't look at spending time at the spa as a luxury, but as required maintenance.

You wouldn't drive an exquisite sports car with dirty oil. And, cheap gas will never give you top performance. So, why treat yourself with any less care? (Repeating this with conviction should quiet any man who is grumbling about the Visa bill.) **Never doubt spending more on your skin than your car. The car you can trade in when it gets old.**

On those glorious occasions when your maintenance is more acute—occupying an entire day at the spa, or involves girlfriends, mimosas, and fluffy terry cloth, those days should be called something more. They are beyond pampering, something like Diva-fying, Princessing, or Sparkling yourself. Isn't that better? Pretty things like diamonds and champagne sparkle, Pampers go on babies' butts and catch poo.

*All things little or big provide opportunities for self-sparkling:*

- Serve yourself. Even if it's takeout, break out the fancy plates. You're at least as special as any guest.
- Wear lingerie that a stripper would be proud of, regardless of what it's hiding under.
- Shopping ~ Little Sparkle: Make three trips to the same store so you'll have more bags.
- Shopping ~ Big Sparkle: New wardrobe. Yes, the whole thing. Sparkling of this magnitude can be blinding.
- Play hooky from work and catch a midday matinee or quickie. The latter requires a hooky companion.
- Go on holiday. Best if you can incorporate several other sparkling items into a great big one.
- Take a limo to the theatre, even the kind with popcorn and Jujus.

# Passports & First Class —two key

elements of ideal City Girl travel. There is no excuse for being without the first, because how can you jet off to Milan if you can't get on the jet? The second makes the getting to and from more pleasurable and far less cramped, but **the going is the important thing, even if your tushie must go coach.**

Traveling is a way to share more of your fabulousness with the rest of the world. Also, it lets you find new stores to shop in. However, one danger of traveling every City Girl faces simply stepping out her door is that her presence may take a bit of the glory away from the scenery.

There are many things to decide once you've decided to travel, but deciding to travel should never be a question. Unless the destination involves icky bugs, icky stores, or visiting people who wouldn't be invited to your parties, traveling is always a good thing to do, and any time is a good time to do it. Even if the trip is only in your mind, take it.

## Quick travel decision reference:

- If the word exotic applies to the place or the boys—yes.
- If the boy of your dreams has tickets in hand and little blue box in his pocket—yes, yes, yes. (Also, a good answer for later.)

*Note: If you ask a City Girl to tend your mail, flora, or fauna while you are away, you will probably return to the fragrance of fresh flowers adorning your hall table. Granted, you may also return to the living room being completely rearranged, but give it a minute. You'll see, it looks better her way. As do most things.*

# Oh, What Bags to Bring?

Once your passport is in hand, the essential element of all travel is wardrobe. There is what you will take there, what you will acquire there, and what you will wear to get there.

For the actual trip, comfortable should be key. Which comfortable is up to you—nonbinding onboard or nonembarrassing on arrival.

*For a City Girl, proper packing consists of four easy steps:*
1. Start with the essentials. *(little black dress)*
2. Add the favorites. *(little black dress)*
3. Predict the unexpected. *(little black dress)*
4. Plan to tip the valet very well. *(big green money)*

Always travel with a bag you can carry. There may be a moment when the valet isn't handy, and schlepping is never attractive. If traveling with a boy, he should also bring a bag he can carry. This is usually larger than he will need, but it creates extra space for you. In case of objections, hold up the items in need of space. These should be of the lacy and skimpy varieties.

For successful City Girl traveling, bring great luggage, but leave the baggage at home. If you choose companions wisely, you'll have ample opportunities to collect memorable moments with devilish details, so why drag along anything un-fun from home?

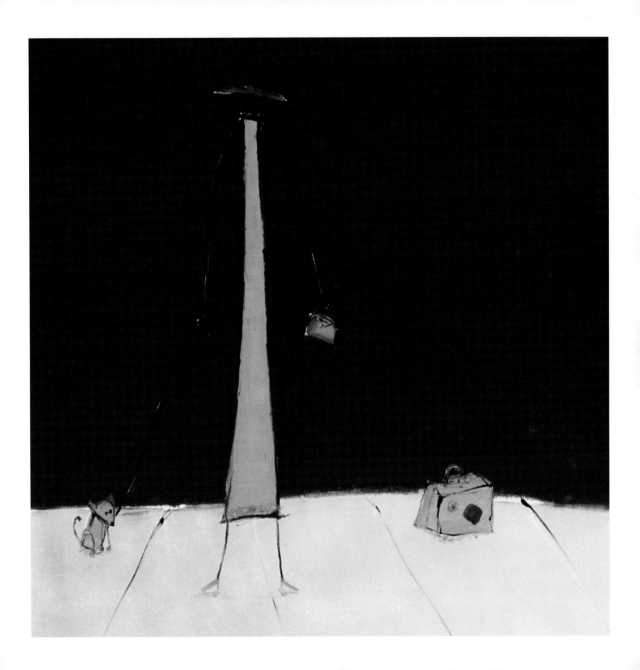

# Who Will Match My Travel Shoes?

*Good criteria to consider for choosing travel companions for any destination:*

- TRAVEL IS ALL ABOUT WARDROBE, and this includes those of a City Girl's companions. If their style and size allows for sharing, it doubles your ensemble selection without doubling your luggage.
- LANGUAGES SPOKEN. Fluency is not needed if useful phrases are known. Such as: *May we see the dessert menu?* And especially helpful, *Thank you for your gushing admiration, but please stop following us down the street on your bicycle.*
- SNORING. This affects the number of rooms, pillows, and drinks needed. It could also affect length of the relationship in general.
- EATING HABITS. Bringing the lactose intolerant to France may not be wise. Also, consider no No-carbers to Italy. Really, the No-carbers are hardly ever fun to eat with, so maybe restrict their company while they are restricting their carbs.
- DEGREE OF WHINING. This should be zero-tolerance policy.
- ABILITY TO DO. Both nothing and lots, at any given time.
- OBSERVATION SKILLS. Girlfriends for spotting cute boys. Boyfriends for not spotting you spotting cute boys.
- SPECIAL COMPANION CRITERIA FOR TROPICAL DESTINATIONS. The view they create on the beach. Regardless of how hot- or not-bodied your accompaniments are, they should sport a flashy attitude, and never flash a Speedo. **(Banana hammocks are a big No-No, regardless of how big the No-No.)**

# To Beach or Not to Beach?

Many decide when to jet, and who to bring, by where they wish to go, but a City girl knows the fun-ness of packing is directly tied to her destination. So, locations should be chosen based on the wardrobe, or lack there of, required.

## Considerations for which bit of the globe you'll be sharing your you-ness with:

CLIMATE: Obviously a wardrobe thing.

- WARM: Less luggage to check, more skin to show.
- HOT: Sweat and humidity factors that wilt silk and poof hair.
- COOL: Cashmere layers so well.
- COLD: Requires parkas and limited shoe selections. So, unless you like your diamonds black, or have a penchant for fur trimming, opt for going below the border, not below zero.

ACTIVITIES: Also a wardrobe thing, a packing thing, and an updated insurance thing.

- Have you ever?
- Are you brilliant at it?
- Do the activities provide for meeting new people?
- Are those people cute boys?
- Does shopping, dining, lounging, and looking fabulous easily fit on the daily itinerary?

SCENERY: Again, wardrobe. Certain natural wonders simply do nothing for your skin tone.

- The same rule applies to countries as cafés—anywhere that doesn't clash with her shoes.
- Does the sightseeing involve boutiques as well as boulders?
- Does the human scenery deserve its own postcard rack?

ADVENTURE: If the term can be applied to the experience or the activities, good thing. If it applies to finding a shower, or eating dinner, approach with caution. And Maalox.

# City Girl on the Go, Go, Go!

A City Girl always has somewhere to be getting to, like a spa appointment, a purse sale, or a party in her honor, and less fun things like work, groceries, or the gym, thus she must consider her means of getting there. The gym has special needs. You may not necessarily look your best on the way to or from, so non-showy transportation modes should be considered.

MODES OF CITY GIRL "HERE TO THERE":

BICYCLES: Helmets and spandex are unfortunate on everyone, but baskets  can be charming and provide a place for your purse.

CHARIOTS DRAWN BY A HANDSOME MAN: Even a skateboard is stylish if navigated by a hot boy.

DRIVE: Anything fast, sleek, sexy, cute, fun, or powerful—basically choose your preferred adjective and clothes to match. Then add a charming key fob, something with diamonds is always nice.

 GOING BY BOAT: A wonderful reason for a new sailing ensemble.

METROS / SUBWAYS / BUSES: When you must, they generally muss.

PIGGYBACK: This transportation mode may not be the daintiest, but it doubles as a flirting activity, and allows you to judge the boost giver's sweeping-off-feet ability.

PLANES: Private, Goodie! First Class, Goodie! Coach, Upgrade!

SCOOTING: Earth-friendly modes of transportation are wonderful, as long as their cool-per-mile is at least as high as the miles-per-gallon.

TAXI (a.k.a Shoe Saver): Think of hailing one as an opportunity to let the masses passing enjoy your presence. A taxi is not quite a limo arrival on the red carpet, but a City Girl can make stepping out of any car a show. Mind the length of your skirt, or your little show could go a little Ho.

TRAINS: Have to love a bar car.

WALK: Only walk on a date if you value the boy more than your shoes.

# Lend a Well-Manicured Hand

A City Girl cares about something besides looking fabulous and finding cute shoes. Finding a cause that stirs your compassion is as important as finding a flattering cut of jeans, but not nearly as difficult. With every cause, disease, and fund having its own ribbon, you're sure to find one to match any outfit. Just be sure you know what your lovely little color stands for, because a City Girl would never don social activism as an accessory—that's what hats are for. A City Girl knows how to pose, but is never a poseur.

Paying attention to what is going on in the world as it orbits around her can have all sorts of benefits for a City Girl. It gives her conversation topics for cute foreign boys she encounters, and knowing political issues can test a date's potential compatibility. You'll quickly see his temper, his debate skills, and his potential of fulfilling your dream of marrying a senator.

## Never don social activism as an accessory, that's what hats are for.

There are many ways to help the world and share a bit of your fabulousness. You can raise money, raise awareness, or raise the roof. Happy hours with a cause are a great way to multitask. The most obvious way for a City Girl to give is to give what she knows so well: style. Donating the results of a healthy closet slimming improves the aesthetics of the population at large, makes you feel even better than you normally do, and creates empty hangers, and you know what that means. Time to shop!

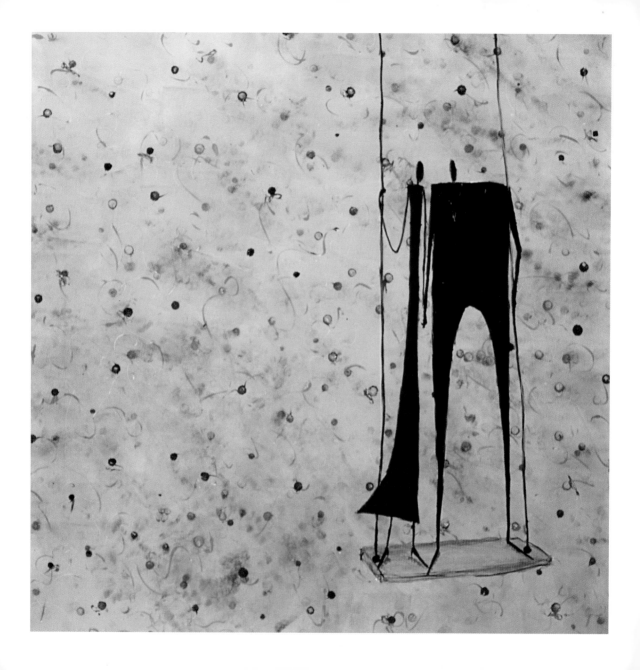

# Love, Dating & Other Things Requiring Heels

When choosing dates, the first thing all City Girls must know is, being pursued is a way of life, not an occasional nicety. So, when you spy a particularity appealing prospect, **let him come to you. Unless the lighting is better on his side of the room.**

In general, think of dating like shopping. Instead of dresses, you're trying on boys. You might think it looks great hanging on the rack, but then it does nothing for you when you get it on. So, shop wisely. Men, unfortunately, don't have handy little price tags or content labels to let us know exactly what we're buying, or how much it's going to cost in emotional currency.

Happily, to help a City Girl find the perfect man, there are a few simple guides to assist in identification.

PERFECT MAN ATTRIBUTES:

- The perfect man is one who won't squint in your spotlight. Very important, considering the spotlight seems to follow a City Girl everywhere she goes.
- Never date a man whose teeth are brighter than his wit. Well, at least not more than one night.
- Also, if a man can't dance standing up, he probably can't dance lying down.
- Is he the perfect kissing height when you're wearing heels? This is determined by you being able to reach him standing flat, or on your toes, or in model pose, or one step up or down.
- If he brings flowers for your date, he gets a gold star. And be sure to have them nicely arranged before breakfast.
- The perfect man will have manners, and use them even in the presence of his buddies. When you find one, compliment his mother. But send his last girlfriend a thank-you note.
- If he speaks constantly about himself, it's fine. As long as it's about how lucky he is to be with you.
- Also important: Who not to choose. You know your date is on the wrong team when you ask him to hold your purse and he asks if he can borrow it.

# Before "Yes"

As for flirting—that vital skill that moves you from finding him to dating him—knowing which result you're going for helps define your success.

- Should he be asking for your number, your Saturday night, your hand?
- Would a little attention be welcome? a.k.a. alleviating boredom?
- Creating jealousy? Potentially dangerous, especially if the one you are making jealous believes in "two can play at that game."
- Justifying the purchase of your clingy pewter camisole? As if looking gorgeous isn't justification enough.

*Once your flirting* prowess has moved you from browsing to buying, there are a number of things to consider before "Yes."

- See him standing up, see him sitting down. Can you distinguish between the two?
- Hear him laugh. If it's like nails on a chalkboard, it and he are unlikely to grow on you.
- Hasn't laughed at anything. Too serious. Only acceptable if you met at a funeral. Or, you think dating someone with no sense of humor will delay developing laugh lines.
- Observe his natural non-date state. If he's Jekyll with you and Hyde with his friends, you could end up married to your dream man's evil twin.
- Run him by The Girls.

 *If a man can't talk to your friends, his shelf life is shorter than sushi.*

- Weigh the "Ooh, he's cute" factor against the "Red flag!" factor. Red flags don't necessarily eliminate the possibility of a date. You don't want to be blind to his faults, but a little time spent with the blinders on can be fun, and acceptable for the short term. However, the long term requires dealing with, ridding of, or bleaching the nasty little things until they are nothing more than a pale, pale pink.

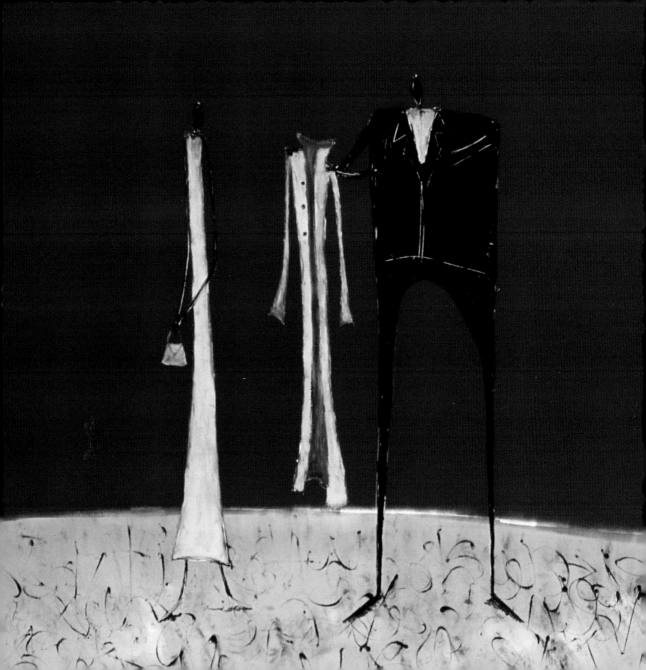

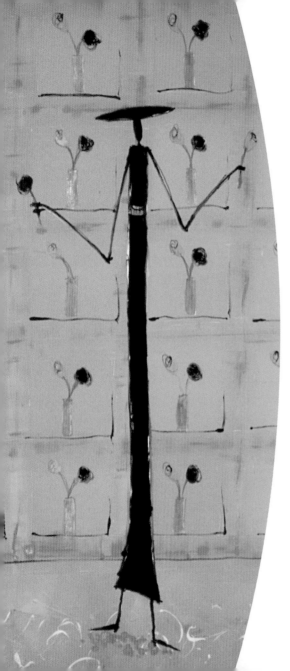

#  "Yes" Again

After any date—good, blah, or regrettable—your friends will inevitably ask everything from, "Do you like him?" to "Did you do him?" A City Girl always has options: Kiss and dish. Kiss and embellish. Kiss and smirk. Your choice will say volumes when it's time to determine if Date One is worthy of a Date Two.

First, was he wise enough to ask for one? Preferably, before the end of the first date he was so lucky to have. Keep in mind, if he waits three days to call, he's not a player—he's just not smart.

*Before "Yes" again, consider the results of "Yes" one:*

- Wasn't bored to tears.
- Laughed to the point of tears.
- He moved up or down on the Hottie Scale.
- Planned a thoughtful date. One that didn't involve a strategically placed TV for viewing of the playoffs while "listening" to you.
- He looked at you like you were candy. And you liked it.
- You're not interested, but you weren't feeling your best, and want to leave a better parting impression.
- You still can't decide if you are, or are not attracted to him, but you have a new pair of shoes that will go perfectly with the restaurant he's suggested.

# Perfect Attire

While choosing attire for dating, follow the Golden Rule: Dress as nicely for others as you'd like others to dress for you. "Casual" should never mean frumpy. "Laid back": Not frumpy. "Hanging out": Still not frumpy. Frumpy is as frumpy looks, and it never looks good on a City Girl.

Eliminating the possibility of accidental frumpy means removing all items that aren't "cute" from your everyday-wear, clean-the-house-wear, and no-one-is-going-to-see-me-wear (the last category being the greatest tempt of fate possible). Wear anything from this category out, and you're sure to run into the gorgeous guy you've been flirting with at the dog park. One step out in frumpy can equal three steps back in flirt.

ALSO REMEMBER: Clingy dresses: *Yes*. Clingy men: *No*.

It's wonderful if they're attentive, and their going MIA is never good, but having enough space between you is vital to your keeping him at all.

*Frumpy is as frumpy looks, and it never looks good on a City Girl.*

Another version of the Golden Rule applies to all things shiny. You can never have too much, except on at one time—it's distracting and tacky. Plus, it makes a boy prematurely nervous about what type, cut, and carat weight of gifts he will be needing to present to you in the future. This is something best taught slowly.

Gold is sparkly and therefore good, but being a Gold Digger refers to a City Girl's approach to her jewelry box, not her relationships. However, if you're going to dig gold, dig big gold. Think Trump with better hair. Much better hair.

# To Have & to Hold

As with cocktails, men should be strong, tall, and smooth, and holding them can be just as tricky.

- HOLDING HIS HAND: This is sweet, and makes you feel young regardless of how long you haven't been getting carded. It's also useful when exiting a limo.
- HOLDING HIS ARM: Casually loop your arm around his elbow. Clutching is not good unless required to not fall, or pretending to be frightened during a movie. (A useful skill for managing his ego and acquiring kisses.)

## As with cocktails, men should be strong, tall, and smooth.

- HOLDING HIS GAZE: Should occur naturally whenever you enter the room. If not, he needs glasses. Things that cling or shoes that put a little extra swing in your backyard help immensely in this area.
- HOLDING HIS MIND: Don't bother holding his if he can't hold yours.
- HOLDING HIS HEART: This is best as a mutually reciprocated situation. When it's not . . . dump, dish, and move on.
- HOLDING CONTROL: Surprisingly easy, as long as you never let him know you have it. Except in bed when black leather is involved. Then make it very, very clear.
- HOLDING HIS ATTENTION: This is similar to his gaze, but requires his brain to be present.
- HOLDING HIS ATTENTION DURING SPORTS: He may look at you with the one eye that's not fixed on the flat screen, but his brain belongs to the remote. Special tactics are generally needed, but even lingerie may not work during playoffs, and full nudity barely registers during championships.

# Holding Me

If a man wants to keep a City Girl holding him, he needs to do some holding of his own.

- First, to be worth holding, he should be able to hold his own martini, literally and figuratively.
- Holding your coat: It makes him look like a gentleman, and is so much more elegant than having to flail your way into a fitted trench.
- Holding your purse: This is rarely vital, but it's a wonderful little test of his chivalry and security in his masculinity. However, if he's nosy or clumsy, this could backfire.
- Holding doors: The general rule in life for a City Girl is whoever gets there first, holds. But this is not applicable for fancy dates, or any time you're wearing something that makes his eyes pop. Then he should do everything he can to get there first. This enhances your impact and the benefit to him: he gets to see you coming and going.

> *Note: If your date is really going for chivalry and wants to open your car door, help him out. Since you are probably carrying a bag that is more accessory than utility, look casual while searching for something among the lipstick and mints, so he can look smooth—hard to do when he scurries.*

- The most important holding a boy can do is you in his arms. It seems to be universal among City Girls that a man is the perfect size (no, not that size) when he can hold you in his arms and you feel "tiny." Quite a feat for a man whose arms are wrapped around brains, beauty, and deadly heels. Clearly, character and biceps can be mutually exclusive.

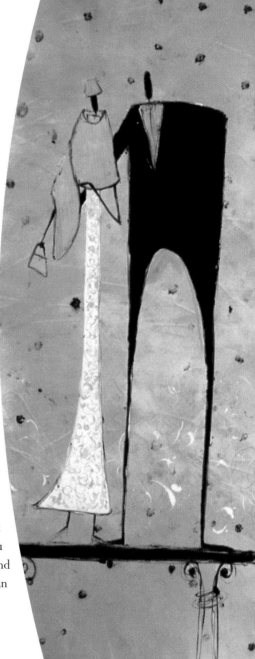

# Boys & Their Egos

In dating, as with any sport involving men, a City Girl should know how to coexist with the male ego. This is a feat equivalent to juggling eggs with a tennis racket, and is best attempted with all your City Girl strengths intact.

ELEMENTS OF DEALING WITH MEN AND THEIR EGOS:

- Regarding giving compliments: Yes, he should. If he deserves them, you should.
- Dealing with his spare tire or his not being able to change one: Be sweet when asking him to correct either. Know how to do the latter, but why risk a fresh manicure when it's not necessary? Besides, it's cute to see your man being all manly. Unless he's just being stubborn, and doesn't actually know how to put the snow chains on, and has wasted two hours of your time on the slopes saying, "You stay warm, I'm almost done."

CONSIDER THESE THINGS BEFORE SAYING ANYTHING THAT COULD BRUISE:

- If the gift he gives you is bigger than the one you've given him, keep him.
- A City Girl's date should always look good. But never better than her shoes.
- You know you're supposed to play hard to get, but sometimes it's more fun to forget.
- When it comes to letting a man win: Your heart, yes. Games and arguments, never. Those he has to win fair and square. You can help him like crazy with the first—after all, you're on the same side in that game.
- On being chased by men: Run slowly. Unless it's a race.
- On chasing men: Only if he's taken your purse.

*If you need a man, a jar lid must be stuck.*
*If you want a man, he's very lucky. Remind him, often.*

# A Generally Fabulous Life

A City Girl's typically fabulous days are filled with all sorts of little things that aren't typically fabulous but quite necessary to keep the rest of her life that way.

Things like errands, exercise, and eye makeup removal. And No! There is no excuse for raccoon eyes. Even if you've been out too late, and the martinis were too many. Even when you're in nature and there are bugs. Even if you have to get up after sex to get ready for bed. Wash the day off your face. And moisturize! **Flaky should describe piecrust, never a City Girl.**

As far as errands go, the word starts with err so that should tell us something. It is a catchall category for anything a City Girl can't fit into fun areas like shopping, dining, or sparkling. While they may be dull to do, you need not be dull while doing them. After all, cute boys need groceries too.

*Thankfully, some daily To-Do's are simply fun to do.*

CHECKING IN WITH THE STARS.

For horoscopes, believe the good, ignore the bad.
(Obviously, someone has misread your moon.)

WANDER THE WEB.

E-mails from friends. Shopping online. Googling a
new boy. What else is the Internet for?

SHINE YOUR FABULOUSNESS.

Learn, grow, and expand—mentally, that is.
A City Girl never stops enhancing her diva-ness.

# Life Beyond Urban

Now, if your daily itinerary (it always sounds better than a To-Do list) has little or no City in your Girl, and your errands are more mall in the burbs than store on the corner, simply look at the food court as a sidewalk café that never has rain.

*Being a City Girl is a state of mind, not a zip code.*

Occasionally, drive around your block twice as if looking for parking. Maybe even complain about the traffic when the parade of minivans and SUVs go by. You see, being a City Girl is a state of mind, not a zip code.

If your suburban is even further sub-urban —a.k.a. "Is that a cow?"—no worries. You really can pull off Prada boots in the pasture. You just may want to pull them off before you go anywhere else.

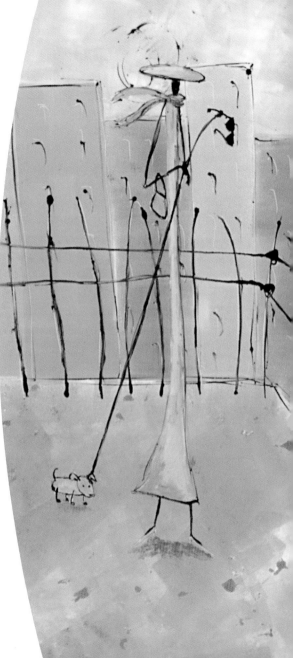

# All things take manners. Especially things that

aren't as fun as buying shoes, or any time you must deal with people who are unaware that all things take manners.

- ACCEPTING COMPLIMENTS: Act surprised, as if you don't get them all the time.
- ACCEPTING GIFTS: *See compliments.*
- ACCEPTING GIFTS YOU DON'T LIKE: Avoid this conundrum by giving your giver a little help. Maybe a small note with the name of, and directions to, the store. Preferred colors, SKU numbers, sizes, and the sales associate's name and direct extension who has everything on hold.
- RETURNING GIFTS: If it's the thought that counts, it counts just as much if you'd rather have it in blue.
- GIFT GIVING: Choose something you'd like yourself, but make sure to get it in their size. And you actually have to give it to be a gift. (Thought doesn't count that much.)

## Screening calls: It's not rude if it keeps you from being rude to whoever is calling.

- KEEPING IN TOUCH: Everyone needs more hugs.
- PARTY FAVORS: Never bring anything you wouldn't drink yourself.
- STANDING OUT: For a City Girl, standing out is not so much an option as a reality. Of course, good manners would say that weddings—not yours, of course—are the one occasion when it is acceptable, nearly expected, for you to not be the most fabulous-looking woman in the room. *Exception: When it's the wedding of an ex. Then manners have little to do with it.*

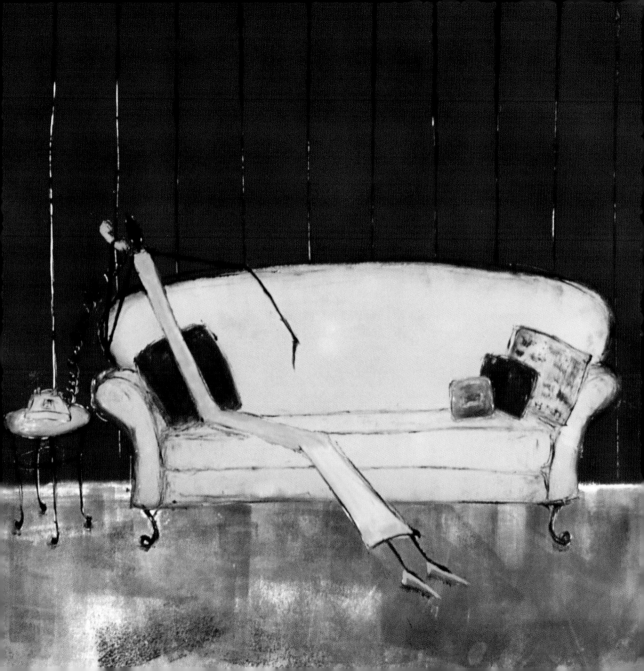

# Staying Fabulous

A credo for any City Girl: Never leave the house without your personality. This includes when finding your fitness, your balance, or your way out into nature.

If your signature color is tangerine, and you always have on something sparkly, why settle for grey, baggy, or dull when you exercise? You'll already be panting and sweating, and while acceptable during sex, it is not the most appealing elsewhere. Happily, sex counts as an exercise. A very fun one.

Choose an exercise activity based on the cuteness of its corresponding clothing. However, if a City Girl's gear has no performance, it has no point. Start with the most important item for the given activity, and coordinate around it. This may require extra shopping, but, oh, well.

- RUNNERS: Match the shoes, from laces to manicure.
- YOGA GIRLS: Luckily, mats are inexpensive, so multi-ensemble away. Clashing is never a good start to your search for inner peace.
- ROCK CLIMBERS: Do whatever it takes to distract from the harness in which no booty looks licious.

Also, all workout attire has a vital function to perform: Sweat Etiquette. There are three elements: (1) It's yours, please keep it. (2) It's called a towel. (3) Color choices that don't show where your workout is working. *Note: Makeup while working out—Bad. Very bad. Save vanity for when you're not sweaty—it's easier to pull off.*

*Never leave the house without your personality.*

There are a myriad of reasons for a City Girl to maintain her stunning self, but she knows exercise in moderation is best. Tone is good, but looking like you're missing a leg on your second X chromosome, is not.

Exercise releases stress which is as important to get rid of as ugly shoes, or frayed underwear.

Big Bonus: Fitness aids in Boy Shopping. You'll attract the sporty ones when in the gym, and everything else when out. And then there is Shopping Shopping. The most important reason for a City Girl to keep her shape and have a fabulously long life—it gives you years more seasons to shop, and you'll look stunning while doing it.

# On the matter of money, the only thing that matters

for a City Girl is that she has her own. She knows it can't buy her happiness, but it can afford her the freedom to pursue her happiness. Of course, a City Girl's current happiness may involve buying spike leather boots that will get her lots of compliments, which makes for happiness.

## Beyond having it, there is what you do with it.

SAVING: There are several types. The first is Paying Less—a.k.a. "On Sale!" It's a City Girl's second favorite thing to hear (the first is any compliment directed at her). When you buy things on sale, you save money. Meaning there's more left in your pocket, and that is somewhat like finding money. And every City Girl knows, more shopping, sushi for lunch, or a facial are always good uses of "found" money.

Next is saving in the form of Not Spending to Start With. This can be a difficult concept when you are faced with a totally funky, shoulder-strap bag in alligator green that is completely different than the same one you have in lizard green.

The not-spending version usually allows for the literal saving version—a.k.a. "In the Bank, Baby." A City Girl lives lavishly within her means, but knows that money in the bank is oh-so-stylish, and big debts are as bad as big hair.

## TREATING & PAYING:

- If you invite—expect to treat.
- If you offer—don't bluff.
- If invited—be able to just in case the invitee is cheap, but don't say "Yes" again.
- If with friends—volleying for the bill tends to come naturally for friends who see each other so often things even out, even when you can't keep track of going out.

BUDGET: A City Girl approaches budgets as a goal, not a limit. Instead of "I can't" it's "I'm saving for a View-of-the-Beach tour of Europe." Having something to smile about when telling yourself you don't need the bag in alligator makes it easier to wave good-bye.

TAXES: Lunches and cocktails are really therapy sessions, and therefore should be fully tax deductible. You're accountant may disagree, but CPAs are notorious for wearing bad shoes.

THE SPLURGE: By far the most fun part of money, and definitely in the self-sparkle category. A true splurge should be used sparingly to retain its yumminess—things like those shoes you simply must have, even if it means you won't be eating out for a month.

*Note: When splurging on the latest that may not last the longest, the price tag should be directly proportioned to the number of wearings you'll be able to squeeze out of it before the trend has trickled. Never spend so much on something that your Visa bill lasts longer than it does.*

# Home, Stunning Home

A City Girl approaches home décor simply—as a very large purse. It holds all her favorite things and should always match her shoes.

## Art should match your personality, not your couch.

In the morning, what you see out your window should be at least as beautiful as what you see in the mirror.

A vase not filled with flowers is like having the shoes without the dress. And there's no such thing as being given too many flowers. **Except carnations, which don't really qualify as flowers.**

# Oh, those silly critics.

Occasionally, even the most fabulous City Girl has to fend off a critic. These are usually others who envy the glow that surrounds her world. They're frustrated that they haven't yet found her perspective on all things beautiful.

The best way to handle one: Give back a sly smile and the sincerest compliment you can find. Even if you have to go so far as "It's so nice, the way your eyes sit on either side of your nose."

Critics in the office tend to come in the form of people who want your job, who think you want theirs, or who think they could do yours even though they can barely do their own. The easiest way to silence the work critic: Be brilliant. Generally simple, being that brilliance comes so naturally to a City Girl.

*The trickiest critic* of all is the self-critic. This one, in the form of the little voices in your head, must be handled with care, and a few simple rules:

1. **If they say something negative, they must be wrong because you're fabulous.**
2. If they're complimentary, they should be agreed with and repeated out loud.
3. If they are saying anything destructive, or suggesting you buy something ugly, they must be completely ignored. Much like men wearing black socks with sandals.
4. The voices can be useful if saying something that inspires you. However, if rule 3 applies to the inspiration, it still applies.
5. If the voices sound at all like your mother, evaluate them using rules 1–4, and then laugh, shoo them away, or call and surprise her with a random act of "Thank you."

On occasion, your little voices are simply holding up a mirror saying, "Excuse me, are we serious?" This is the wonderful thing about a City Girl—she is fully aware of her princessness and knows that, on occasion, even she can go too far. Always remember, being able to laugh at yourself as much as others is vital to living fabulously in your City Girl world.

# Au Revoir

Now that you know when not to wear beige—ever—and that carnations don't count, there's one last thing a City Girl must always remember. In life, as in fashion, **Never settle. Period.** Whether it's romance, lunch, or the fit of your shoes, you are fabulous and the world orbiting around you should be too. You can choose to let loose your inner City Girl-ness in tiny bits, just a sparkle here and there, or uncork it and pour like good wine on sale. Either way, a City Girl is lavish with herself and others. Especially when it comes to giving compliments, sharing advice, taxis, cocktails, or kisses, and loving all things shiny.

## Time to go shopping!

So, off you go to color-coordinate your very own fabulous world, and flaunt your City Girl regardless of your bank account, zip code, finger status, or amount of closet space. (There's no need to worry that yours isn't enough. You simply can't have too much, so no one ever really has enough.) And remember, when you encounter another as divine as yourself, share the good lighting.

# Thank you, thank you, thank you.

To all the princesses I've giggled and awed at. (Yes, I put them first so not to hear them whine.)

To all the beautiful City Girls it is my pleasure to know and share cookies and wine with.

To the boys who are enough girl to point out bad shoes. Olives, thanks again for brunch.

To Squirrel & Lil' C who let Auntie see dreams and COO for being "Pret' near retired."

To the ones who believe I can fly and the Golden Child for leaving space in the attic.

To those who help me find my wings and the ones who tell me where the commas go.

*Chase your dreams. When you catch them, run faster, and make them keep up with you.*

— karn